The Confederate
States of America

PETER BENOIT

Children's Press®
An Imprint of Scholastic Inc.
New York Toronto London Auckland Sydney
Mexico City New Delhi Hong Kong
Danbury, Connecticut

Content Consultant
James Marten, PhD
Professor and Chair, History Department
Marquette University
Milwaukee, Wisconsin

Library of Congress Cataloging-in-Publication Data

Benoit, Peter, 1955–
  The Confederate States of America/Peter Benoit.
      p. cm. — (A true book)
  Includes bibliographical references and index.
  ISBN-13: 978-0-531-26310-5 (lib. bdg.)   ISBN-10: 0-531-26310-X (lib. bdg.)
  ISBN-10: 978-0-531-26623-6 (pbk.)   ISBN-10: 0-531-26623-0 (pbk.)
  1. Confederate States of America—History—Juvenile literature. 2. United States—History—Civil
War, 1861–1865—Juvenile literature. I. Title.
  E487.B46 2012
  973.7'13—dc22   2011011968

All rights reserved. Published in 2012 by Children's Press, an imprint of Scholastic Inc.
Printed in China 62
SCHOLASTIC, CHILDREN'S PRESS, A TRUE BOOK, and associated logos are trademarks and/or registered trademarks of Scholastic Inc.
7 8 9 10 R 21 20 19 18 17

Scholastic Inc., 557 Broadway, New York, NY 10012.

Find the Truth!

Everything you are about to read is true *except* for one of the sentences on this page.

Which one is **TRUE**?

T or F The Confederate States of America were formed before President Abraham Lincoln took office.

T or F Confederate president Jefferson Davis was executed after the Civil War.

Find the answers in this book.

3

Contents

THE **BIG** TRUTH!

Slavery in the South

**Enslaved
African
Americans**

Confederate generals

3 The Confederate Government

4 The End of an Era

The Confederate States of America issued its first currency in April 1861.

ONE HUNDRED DOLLARS

Confederate States America

South Carolina's secession began a series of events that led to the creation of the Confederate States of America.

CHAPTER 1

Seeds of Secession

The state of South Carolina **seceded** from the United States of America on December 20, 1860. This set off a chain of events that led to 11 states leaving the Union to form a new nation called the Confederate States of America. South Carolina's decision to leave the Union was not made suddenly. It happened after years of disagreement between the northern and southern states about how the country should be run.

Secessionists created new flags to show support for states' rights.

Rural villages were much more common than larger cities and towns in the early years of the United States.

States' Rights

Americans had disagreed for years over which powers should belong to the states and which should belong to the **federal** government. These differences did not cause major problems at first. Most of the country's settlements consisted of farms and small villages. People from different states did not often communicate with one another.

This lack of communication led to the states creating their own rules and developing in their own ways. Each state passed laws that suited its people and **economy**. The federal government did not often take part in this process. Most southern states' economies were based on agriculture. Some farms were small. But others were large **plantations**. They produced crops such as cotton, sugar, and tobacco.

Before the Civil War, Louisiana produced between 25 and 50 percent of all sugar used in the United States.

Trade and Slavery

The economy in the South depended on two things to make it work. The first was trade with foreign countries. Great Britain purchased huge amounts of cotton and tobacco from the southern states. The second was slavery. Slavery was important because southern farmers and plantation owners relied on slaves to produce their crops. Slavery was not allowed in most of the northern states. But millions of slaves were forced to work on southern farms.

Slaves were forced to do difficult, tiring jobs such as picking cotton.

The U.S. slave population was more than four million by the beginning of the Civil War.

As printing presses became more widely available, they changed the way people communicated.

Changing Times

Advances in communication and transportation began to have major effects on the country in the early 1800s. Railroads and the printing press made it easy for people to learn what was happening across the country. People began to develop opinions about the other states' ways of doing things. The federal government eventually started to take a more active role in the country's lawmaking process.

Tariff Trouble

The U.S. government created a new **tariff** on imported goods in 1828. It had previously been cheaper to import goods from foreign countries than to get the same goods from the manufacturers in the northern United States. The tariff was designed to protect these U.S. companies from going out of business. The results of the tariff eventually harmed the southern agricultural economy.

Tariffs were designed to help U.S. manufacturing businesses by making foreign-manufactured goods more expensive.

The tariffs made it hard for plantation owners to sell their crops.

Many southerners called the tariff "The Tariff of Abominations."

People in the southern states were now forced to purchase more expensive goods from the north. Manufacturers in countries such as Great Britain began to lose money as Americans purchased fewer of their products. This left foreign nations with less money to buy crops from the southern states. The southerners feared that this would hurt their economy as time went on.

The Nullification Crisis

Protests from the south led to the U.S. government lowering the tariff in 1832. But this did not satisfy all southerners. The South Carolina state government passed the Ordinance of **Nullification**. It stated that the tariffs would not apply in that state. It also threatened that the

U.S. vice president John C. Calhoun spoke out in favor of nullification.

state would secede if the U.S. government tried to force them to pay the tariff. No other states joined South Carolina in this protest. State leaders were pressured into canceling it.

Regional Tensions

South Carolina's actions showed that there was a large difference between northern and southern states. The issue of slavery divided the North and South even further over the next 25 years. New territories were added to the western part of the country. There was debate on whether or not to allow slavery in those locations. Many people in the north were against slavery. The South believed that the North was attacking its slave-based economy.

After the Civil War, Senator Sumner supported the right for former slaves to vote.

In 1856, South Carolina congressman Preston S. Brooks attacked Massachusetts senator Charles Sumner with a cane over a disagreement about states' rights.

CHAPTER 2

The Birth of the Confederate States of America

The Confederate States of America was often called simply the Confederacy. It was born out of the southern fear of **abolition**. Abolitionists hoped to do away with slavery completely. Abolitionists and southern slaveholders had totally different beliefs. William Lloyd Garrison was the editor of an abolitionist newspaper called the *Liberator*. Garrison wrote that he was filled with "indignation

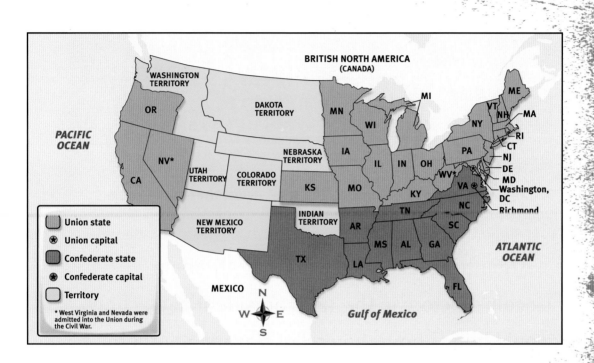

This map shows the Union and Confederate states during the Civil War (1861–1865).

and abhorrence" at "that which turns a man into a thing." But U.S. representative Alexander Stephens of Georgia described slavery as a "natural and normal condition."

Abraham Lincoln's election was the final event that made some southern states secede from the Union.

Southern leaders feared that Abraham Lincoln's victory in the 1860 presidential election would bring about the end of slavery. Southern slaveholders had previously had a controlling influence in the Supreme Court. They also had powerful backing in Congress. The South believed Lincoln's election would put control in the hands of those who were against slavery. Some states believed secession was the only way to preserve slavery against the threat of the abolitionists.

Support for secession was divided. Extremists such as Alabama congressman William Lowndes Yancey threatened secession if Lincoln won the election. Such extremists were known as Fire-Eaters. Other groups took a more moderate position. They wished to avoid secession until all slave states agreed. A mixture of Union supporters and secessionists helped prevent secession plans in some border states.

Yancey later served as a Confederate diplomat to Europe during the Civil War.

William Lowndes Yancey was one of the most public supporters of secession.

South Carolina led the way toward secession. It started by denying the power of federal judges in their state. Then its two U.S. senators quit. South Carolina seceded from the Union on December 20, 1860. Mississippi, Florida, Alabama, Georgia, Louisiana, and Texas had

Jefferson Davis was the first and only president of the Confederacy.

all followed by February 1861. **Delegates** from the seven states formed the Confederate States of America. Former Mississippi senator Jefferson Davis was named president of the Confederacy.

The Cornerstone Speech

On March 21, 1861, Confederate vice president Alexander Stephens delivered his famous Cornerstone Speech in Savannah, Georgia. He spoke about differences between the U.S. federal government and the Confederacy. Among them was the attitude about the "peculiar institution" of slavery. He claimed that the Confederacy was founded "upon the great truth that the Negro is not equal to the white man." Stephens owned about three dozen slaves.

Lincoln took office on March 4, 1861. U.S. troops at Fort Sumter in Charleston, South Carolina, requested supplies shortly afterward. Fort Sumter was one of the few remaining Union military bases on Confederate soil. Lincoln notified South Carolina governor Francis Pickens of the operation. But Pickens suspected that Lincoln would try to send weapons and troops. The Confederates attacked the fort on April 12.

The attack on Fort Sumter marked the beginning of the Civil War.

No one died during the attack on Fort Sumter.

Volunteer soldiers helped strengthen the Union army.

Fort Sumter surrendered. Lincoln called on state **militias** to volunteer for federal service and help reclaim federal property. States on the border of the Union and Confederate territories were put in a difficult position. The Confederacy would consider it an attack if they joined their militias to the Union forces. These states refused Lincoln's request. Virginia, Tennessee, North Carolina, and Arkansas joined the Confederacy. The American Civil War had begun.

Slavery in the South

Millions of enslaved Africans were forced to work on southern plantations during the height of slavery in the United States. At one point, about 40 percent of all people living in the South were slaves. Slaves often lived and worked in poor conditions. They were treated harshly if they disobeyed their owners.

Resistance and Punishment

Some slaves defied their masters by working slowly, breaking tools, or refusing to work at all. Slaves were often whipped or tortured for this.

Destroyed Families

Slaves were bought and sold at their owners' will. Many slave families were separated. Owners sometimes did this to punish slaves.

The Underground Railroad

Slaves often attempted to escape. Northerners often helped slaves escape to freedom in northern states or Canada. The routes were known as the Underground Railroad.

CONSTITUTION

CONFEDERATE STATES OF AMERICA.

———◆●◆———

WE, the people of the Confederate States, each State acting in its sovereign and independent character, in order to form a permanent federal government, establish justice, insure domestic tranquillity, and secure the blessings of liberty to ourselves and our posterity—invoking the favor and guidance of Almighty God—do ordain and establish this Constitution for the Confederate States of America.

ARTICLE I.

SECTION 1.

All legislative powers herein delegated shall be vested in a Congress of the Confederate States, which shall consist of a Senate and House of Representatives.

SECTION 2.

1. The House of Representatives shall be composed of members chosen every second year by the people of the several States; and the electors in each State shall be citizens of the Confederate States, and have the qualifications requisite for electors of the most numerous branch of the State Legislature; but no person of foreign birth, not a citizen of the Confederate States, shall be allowed to vote for any officer, civil or political, State or Federal.

2. No person shall be a Representative who shall not have attained the age of twenty-five years, and be a citizen of the Confederate States, and who shall not, when elected, be an inhabitant of that State in which he shall be chosen.

The Confederate
Constitution was based
mainly on the U.S.
Constitution.

CHAPTER 3

The Confederate Government

The Confederacy had its own constitution. Slavery was upheld. Protective tariffs were forbidden. The Confederate Constitution also guaranteed the rights of all slave owners. Unlike the U.S. government, the Confederacy did not allow money raised from taxes in one state to be spent on improvements for a different state.

 The Confederate Constitution was signed by 44 representatives from seven states.

Howell Cobb, the president of the Confederate Congress, was a former U.S. Speaker of the House.

The Confederate Congress was very similar to the U.S. Congress.

The Confederate president would be elected to one six-year term. Reelection was not allowed. The Confederate Constitution also established a **legislature** with two houses. The Senate was made up of two senators from each of the 11 Confederate states. There were also two each from Kentucky and Missouri. These two states were not part of the Confederacy. But they both had populations that showed significant Confederate support.

The Confederate Congress had a House of Representatives with 109 members. It also contained a small number of Native American delegates. They were not allowed to vote. State legislatures chose senators, and voters elected the representatives. The Confederacy did not have a supreme court. It used a local court system instead. District judges and state courts continued to operate as they had before.

The first Confederate White House was located in Montgomery, Alabama.

Thomas "Stonewall" Jackson earned his nickname by holding back Union forces at the Battle of Bull Run in 1861.

A Capital in Motion

For a short time, the Confederate capital was located in Montgomery, Alabama. In May 1861, it was relocated to Richmond, Virginia. It remained there until the final week of the Civil War. It was then moved again to Danville, Virginia. The Confederacy maintained its own army, navy, and marines. These military forces were put to use almost immediately when the Civil War broke out shortly after the Confederacy formed.

A Shortage of Soldiers

By April 16, 1862, Confederate leaders had decided that it would be necessary to require all men between the ages of 18 and 35 to serve in the military. But **desertion** was a constant problem. Certain groups of people, such as planters, were excused from joining. The system became dishonest. Confederate states sometimes refused to supply troops. They used states' rights as an excuse.

Diplomacy

The Confederacy printed its own paper money and had its own national flag. The Confederacy tried to win recognition and support throughout Europe for its war with the United States. Numerous European countries were sympathetic to the Confederacy. But President Lincoln warned Europe that support for the Confederacy meant war with the United States.

Like the U.S. flag, the Confederate national flag had a star for each state.

More stars were added to the Confederate flag as more states joined the Confederacy.

Some Confederate money featured pictures of slaves working in fields.

Inflation

Diplomacy was failing. The Confederacy applied economic pressure to Europe by slowing exports of cotton. But the Confederate war effort was doomed without the money that came from cotton sales. The Confederacy began printing large amounts of paper money to pay for its expenses. This caused severe **inflation**. The Confederate dollar had almost no value by the end of the war. The South's economy was badly damaged.

Confederate general
Robert E. Lee was forced to
surrender once he realized
that his shrinking forces
had no chance at victory.

CHAPTER 4

The End of an Era

Hundreds of thousands of lives on both sides were lost during the four years of fighting in the Civil War. The Confederacy had failed to gain recognition. Confederate general Robert E. Lee surrendered to Union general Ulysses S. Grant at Appomattox Court House in Virginia on April 9, 1865. This made victory a sure thing for the Union. But what exactly caused the Confederacy's defeat?

← Appomattox Court House became a national historic monument in 1940.

Economic Issues

The odds of winning the war were immediately against the Confederacy because of the Union's economic superiority. The Confederacy had the advantage of its enormous agricultural production. But the Northern states had more than twice the Confederacy's population and more than three times its wealth. Northern states also had a far more developed railroad system and much more manufacturing.

Timeline of the Confederacy

1828

The U.S. government places a high tariff on imported goods.

1860

South Carolina secedes from the Union.

The Confederacy also failed to defend its territory throughout the war. The Union forces attacked Southern territory and destroyed important resources. The Confederate forces hoped to convince the Union that the cost of war was too great to continue fighting. They believed that Union support for the war would disappear when Lincoln's term as president ended. These hopes were crushed when Lincoln was reelected in 1864.

1861
Confederate troops fire on Fort Sumter.

1865
The Confederacy is defeated in the Civil War.

No Support From Europe

The Confederacy's failure to gain the support of France and Great Britain also contributed to its downfall. It came close to gaining Great Britain's help because of the two countries' economic importance

British prime minister Henry John Temple believed that Great Britain should stay neutral during the Civil War.

to one another. But Union diplomats were able to convince the Europeans to stay out of the war. This denied the Confederates valuable resources and military assistance.

Leadership Weakness?

Some historians believe that the Confederacy's biggest problem was a lack of good military leaders. Generals such as Stonewall Jackson and James Longstreet were excellent at leading smaller groups of soldiers. But they were unable to successfully manage the huge numbers of forces they commanded during the Civil War. General Robert E. Lee showed military genius and dynamic leadership. But this was not enough to carry the entire Confederate war effort.

Lee's father was a close friend of George Washington's.

Despite his considerable leadership skills, Robert E. Lee was not able to win the war.

Other historians point to disagreements between Confederate leaders as a major problem. Jefferson Davis was known for being stubborn. Vice President Stephens often disagreed with him publicly. Conflicts such as these may prevent any government from working smoothly. Confederate leaders did not make fast decisions when they were needed. They often argued over how to proceed.

Davis fled south from the capital when he heard of Lee's surrender at Appomattox.

Jefferson Davis did not have the leadership skills needed to run a new nation effectively.

Confederate military leaders often had trouble getting their men to follow orders because of Southern belief in individualism.

Too Much Freedom

The Confederates' strong belief in individual freedom may have contributed to their defeat as well. Members of the Confederate military would sometimes refuse to follow orders from superior officers. Many saw Davis's decision to require military service as an attempt to destroy states' rights. The Confederacy lacked the two-party political system of the Union. This meant that few alternatives to Davis's policies were put forward.

Davis received offers of free defense from multiple Northern lawyers.

Jefferson Davis never received a proper trial for his crimes.

After the War

The Confederate government officially ended on May 5, 1865. Five days later, Davis was captured, charged with treason (helping the enemy during war), and imprisoned. He was released after two years. The war was costly for both the Northern and Southern states. It took years to rebuild the bonds between them. There is still disagreement to this day about states' rights. But people have come to rely on political debate instead of secession to achieve their goals. ★

First state to secede from the Union: South Carolina

Number of Confederate states: 11

Confederate president's length of term: 6 years

Number of houses in Confederate legislature: 2

Number of men elected to Confederate House of Representatives: 109

Date of Confederate attack on Fort Sumter: April 12, 1861

Ages of men required to serve in Confederate military: 18 to 35

Years Civil War was fought: 1861 to 1865

Place where the South surrendered to the Union: Appomattox Court House, Virginia

Length of the Confederacy's existence: Less than 5 years

Did you find the truth?

T The Confederate States of America were formed before President Abraham Lincoln took office.

F Confederate president Jefferson Davis was executed after the Civil War.

Resources

Books

Aretha, David. *Jefferson Davis*. New York: Chelsea House, 2009.

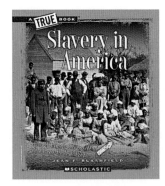

Blashfield, Jean F. *Slavery in America*. New York: Children's Press, 2012.

Collins, Terry. *Robert E. Lee: The Story of the Great Confederate General*. Mankato, MN: Capstone Press, 2011.

Gillis, Jennifer Blizin. *The Confederate Soldier*. Minneapolis: Compass Point Books, 2007.

Grant, R. G. *Slavery: Real People and Their Stories of Enslavement*. New York: DK Publishing, 2009.

Olson, Kay Melchisedech. *The Terrible, Awful Civil War*. Mankato, MN: Capstone Press, 2010.

Somervill, Barbara A. *Women of the Confederacy*. Minneapolis: Compass Point Books, 2007.

Williams, Jean Kinney. *Jefferson Davis: President of the Confederacy*. Minneapolis: Compass Point Books, 2005.

Organizations and Web Sites

History.com — Jefferson Davis

www.history.com/topics/jefferson-davis
Learn more about the life and accomplishments of the only president of the Confederate States of America.

PBS — Map: The Confederate States of America

www.pbs.org/civilwar/war/map1.html
Check out a map of the Confederate states and read more about the Civil War.

Places to Visit

Appomattox Court House National Historical Park

Highway 24, PO Box 218
Appomattox, VA 24522
(434) 352-8987 ext. 26
www.nps.gov/apco/index.htm
Take a tour of the historic site where Confederate general Robert E. Lee surrendered to Union general Ulysses S. Grant.

Fort Sumter National Monument

1214 Middle Street
Sullivan's Island, SC 29482
(843) 883-3123
www.nps.gov/fosu/index.htm
Walk the grounds where the first shots of the Civil War were fired and view one of the best collections of 19th-century seacoast artillery anywhere in the United States.

Important Words

abolition (ab-uh-LIH-shuhn)—the official end of something

delegates (DEL-i-gitz)—people who represent other people at a meeting or in a legislature

desertion (di-ZUR-shuhn)—to run away from the army

diplomacy (duh-PLOH-muh-see)—establishing relations between different countries

economy (i-KON-uh-mee)—the way a country runs its industry, trade, and finance

federal (FED-ur-uhl)—a several states united under and controlled by one central power

inflation (in-FLAY-shuhn)—a general increase in prices

legislature (LEJ-is-lay-chur) —a group of people who have the power to make or change the laws of a country or state

militias (muh-LISH-uhz)—groups of people who are trained to fight but who aren't professional soldiers

nullification (nuh-lih-fih-KAY-shuhn)—to have canceled or made of no value

plantations (plan-TAY-shuhnz)—large farms found in warm climates

seceded (si-SEED-id)—withdrew formally from a group or an organization

tariff (TA-rif)—a tax on goods that are imported or exported

Index

Page numbers in **bold** indicate illustrations

About the Author

Peter Benoit is educated as a mathematician but has many other interests. He has taught and tutored high school and college students for many years, mostly in math and science. He also runs summer workshops for writers and students of literature. Mr. Benoit has also written more than 2,000 poems. His life has been one committed to learning. He lives in Greenwich, New York.